Institutional Racism and the Police: Fact or Fiction?

Institutional Racism and the Police: Fact or Fiction?

David G. Green (Editor)
John G.D. Grieve & Julie French
Michael Ignatieff
Mike O'Brien
Robert Skidelsky

Institute for the Study of Civil Society
London

First published August 2000

ISBN 1-903 386-06-3

Typeset by the Institute for the Study of Civil Society
in New Century Schoolbook

Printed in Great Britain by
The Cromwell Press
Trowbridge, Wiltshire

Contents

The Authors

Julie French was the Senior Family Liaison Officer within the Racial and Violent Crime Task Force, supervising the implementation of family liaison policy within the Metropolitan Police Service (MPS). She joined the MPS in 1995, serving for two years at South Norwood Division in various operational posts. In 1998 she was seconded to a strategic unit responding to the findings of the Public Inquiry into the Death of Stephen Lawrence before joining the Racial and Violent Crime Task Force in 1999. She has a BSc (Hons.) degree in managerial and administrative studies (Aston University), a four-year course that included a placement in New York.

David G. Green is the Director of the Institute for the Study of Civil Society. His books include *Power and Party in an English City*, Allen & Unwin, 1980; *Mutual Aid or Welfare State?*, Allen & Unwin, 1984 (with L. Cromwell); *Working-Class Patients and the Medical Establishment*, Temple Smith/ Gower, 1985; *The New Right: The Counter Revolution in Political, Economic and Social Thought*, Wheatsheaf, 1987; *Reinventing Civil Society*, IEA, 1993; *Community Without Politics*, IEA, 1996; *Benefit Dependency*, IEA, 1998; *An End to Welfare Rights*, IEA, 1999; and *Delay, Denial and Dilution*, IEA, 1999 (with L. Casper).

He wrote the chapter on 'The Neo-Liberal Perspective' in *The Student's Companion to Social Policy*, Blackwell, 1998.

John G.D. Grieve is Deputy Assistant Commissioner of the Metropolitan Police, which he joined in 1966 at Clapham. He has served as detective in South London and has worked in every role from undercover officer to policy chair on drug squads over a 30-year period. His duties have also involved the Flying Squad (two tours of duty),

vi

Robbery Squad and Murder Squads including East London Area Major Investigation Pool. He was a Divisional Commander at Bethnal Green in East London. He has an honours degree in philosophy and psychology (Newcastle University) and a master's degree post graduate research in drugs policy analysis from Cranfield University, travelling on a Swiss charitable scholarship throughout Europe. DAC Grieve has worked in Europe, America, South East Asia and Australia. He introduced Asset Seizure Investigation in the United Kingdom and was Head of Training at Hendon Police College. During that time he organised the Community, Fairness, Justice Conference. He was the first Director of Intelligence for the Metropolitan Police, led the MPS Intelligence Project and the Anti-Terrorist Squad as National Co-ordinator during the 1996-1998 bombing campaigns. DAC Grieve was appointed Director of the first Racial and Violent Crime Task Force in August 1998. His interests include walking, history (including art and police history) and painting. He was awarded the QPM in 1997 and the CBE in the millennium honours list.

Michael Ignatieff gained a doctorate in history at Harvard and has held academic posts at King's College, Cambridge, St Antony's College, Oxford, the University of California at Berkeley, the University of London and the London School of Economics. His books include *A Just Measure of Pain: Penitentiaries in the Industrial Revolution*, *The Russian Album* and *Virtual War: Kosovo and Beyond*. Screenplays include *1991* and *Eugene Onegin* as well as the television play *Dialogue in the Dark*, directed by Jonathan Miller. He was writer and presenter of a six-part documentary series on nationalism entitled *Blood and Belonging*, which was shown on BBC2, CBC and PBS and he hosted the flagship BBC TV arts programme *The Late Show*. His columns appear in *The Observer, The New Republic, The New Yorker, Harpers, Time International* and *Prospect,* and he is currently teaching at the Carr Centre for Human Rights at the Kennedy School, Harvard.

Mike O'Brien was appointed Parliamentary Under Secretary of State at the Home Office on 5 May 1997. He was educated at Blessed Edward Oldcorne School, Worcester Technical College and North Staffordshire Polytechnic. Member of Parliament for Warwickshire North since 1992, Mr O'Brien was opposition spokesman on Treasury and economic affairs from 1995 and the city spokesman from September 1996 until the general election. He is a former chairman of the Backbench Home Affairs Committee and has also been a member of two Commons Select Committees: Home Affairs (1992-1994) and Treasury and Civil Service (1993-1995). Mr O'Brien is also a former parliamentary adviser to the Police Federation. He lectured in law for six years before working as a solicitor until April 1992 when he was elected MP. He is married with two young daughters.

Robert Skidelsky is Chairman of the Social Market Foundation and Professor of Political Economy at Warwick University. He is the definitive biographer of the economist John Maynard Keynes, the third volume of which is due for publication in November. His wide-ranging areas of expertise include higher education, the economy, the school curriculum and foreign affairs. His spirited opposition to Government policy on Kosovo led to his dismissal by William Hague as principal opposition Front Bench spokesman in the House of Lords on Treasury affairs.

Foreword

The Macpherson report was a watershed in British race relations and has led to the adoption of policies by the Metropolitan Police and the Home Office which are described below by John Grieve and the Home Office Minister, Mike O'Brien. In the hope of encouraging a more enlightened public debate, the Institute for the Study of Civil Society is simultaneously publishing two books containing a range of strongly-held views on the subject.

Macpherson's claim that the Metropolitan Police were guilty of 'institutional racism' provoked considerable controversy at the time of publication and continues to be strongly disputed, as the contributions to this book by Lord Skidelsky and Michael Ignatieff show.

Institutional Racism and the Police is published as a companion volume to a major study by Norman Dennis, George Erdos and Ahmed Al-Shahi, *Racist Murder and Pressure Group Politics*, which dissects the Macpherson report and challenges its approach.

David G. Green

The Age of Inequality

Robert Skidelsky

It is alarming, and deeply depressing, that the inquiry into the murder of Stephen Lawrence, chaired by Sir William Macpherson, should so quickly have achieved the status of Holy Writ, despite some spirited pockets of journalistic resistance. For while palpably well-intentioned, the Report may do more harm than good. And this for two reasons. It has firmly inserted the slippery concepts of 'institutional' and 'unwitting' racism into public discourse, from where they will be very difficult to dislodge, and which will inhibit clear thought on race relations. And by concentrating attention on the racial aspects of the murder and its investigation, it diverts attention from the real lesson of the inquiry, which is the urgent need to improve the quality of the police service for all people, white as well as black, who lack the position, power and wealth to command proper attention when they are victims of crimes.

This is not, in any way, to impugn the motives or efforts of the Lawrence family and their legal team to expose the inadequacy of the service they received. They were rottenly treated. Indeed, without the extraordinary determination of Mr and Mrs Lawrence, their son's murder would have remained just another unresolved crime with the police bungling hidden from public view. From their point of view police incompetence had one obvious explanation:

This chapter first appeared in *The Review*, Journal of the Social Market Foundation, August 1999, and is reproduced by kind permission.

racism. The Report has satisfied them on this. It hopes it may be 'cathartic'. But having read the Report I am not convinced this is the right conclusion; and it is only achieved by expanding the definition of racism so far that it is invulnerable to falsification. Politics and truth came into conflict, and politics won.

Basically, the Report seeks to explain the incompetent police investigation into Stephen Lawrence's murder by the existence of 'institutional racism' in the Metropolitan Police Service. It accepts, that is, the 'chilling' contention of Lawrence's parents and their legal advisers, while rejecting the 459 page Report of the Police Complaints Authority that there was: 'no evidence to support the finding of racist conduct by any Metropolitan Police Officer involved in the investigation of the murder of Stephen Lawrence'.[1]

Before turning to what the Report means by 'institutional' or 'unwitting' racism, it is important to point out its place in the structure of the Report. The chapter on 'Racism', which tries to define these terms, runs from pages 20-35 of the 335 pages of text. It is not the conclusion to which the evidence leads, but the premise of the enquiry. The reader is constantly invited to interpret the detailed evidence concerning the police investigation, set out in the following 37 chapters, in light of the theoretical analysis of 'Racism' advanced at the start of the Report. The Report's typical method is to deal with the activities of the officers involved, record their deficiencies—often palpable, though sometime rendered so by hindsight—and conclude, wherever possible, that 'unwitting racism' must have been responsible for their errors.

The conclusion to which reading the document irresistibly leads—if I may borrow one of the Report's favourite phrases—is that the judge and his advisers knew from the start that this was how they were going to interpret the botched police investigation, in the wider interest, as they conceived it, of better race relations.

The definition of racism, which Chapter 6 reaches, after a long and meandering discussion, is that it is anything perceived to be racist. The perpetrators of racist activity may not know they are racist at all. All they have to do to be so called is to treat people in a way which is interpreted as being racist. Racism, in short, is insensitivity to the feelings of members of ethnic minorities. It is a cultural failure. The Metropolitan Police Service caused offence to the black community and therefore was 'institutionally racist'. The Report only just falls short of dubbing the Commissioner of the Metropolitan Police an unwitting racist for denying that his force was institutionally racist. 'We assert again that there must be an unequivocal acceptance that the problem actually exists as a prerequisite to addressing it successfully',[2] it sternly proclaims.

The notion that the perception of a fact makes it a fact is a legal and philosophical monstrosity. If it is proposed, as indeed the Report does, to make unwitting racism a legal offence, the only evidence relevant to a judgment about whether an admitted word or act constituted an offence would be the assertion by the plaintiff that an offence had been committed. The Report is true to its principles. Thus from the fact that Police Constable Joanne Smith described Duwayne Brooks, who had been with Stephen Lawrence when he was stabbed, as 'irate and aggressive'—he called her 'a f****** c***'—the Report deduces that: 'Mr Brooks was stereotyped as a young black man exhibiting unpleasant hostility and agitation'.[3] The Report, in fact, makes it clear that Duwayne Brooks was badly and insensitively treated. But the fact that his police 'handlers' did not know how to handle him, does not, on any common-sense reading, make them racists.

The Report leads us through a maze of bungling and incompetence, starting with the failure to order the early arrest of the five suspects, and continuing through all kinds of lapses of judgment, failure to follow proper procedures, delay in following up clues, and so on. However, three features of the story struck this reader. First, most of the poor police work was just that—the product of an under-staffed, under-equipped, and above all, a low calibre force. When officers arrived on the scene of the crime to find Stephen Lawrence dying, none of them knew how to give him first aid. This, one would have thought, is a far more serious defect than their lack of training in race awareness. The mistakes in the investigation do not require a racist explanation. I do not believe that, if a poor white youth had been murdered in that area, the results would have been any better. Of course, if a prominent person, of any race, had been murdered, a much higher-quality investigation would have been mounted. Jill Dando's killer will be pursued much more relentlessly and effectively than Stephen Lawrence's murderers were. It is curious that the inquiry never considered social class as a possible explanation of the poor police performance. Poor people, or neighbourhoods, get poor service, whatever their race.

Second, although the Report is eager to nail racism as the cause of the police failure to secure a trial, much less a conviction, for the murder of Stephen Lawrence, the incidents of race insensitivity it adduces were not—except possibly in the treatment of Duwayne Brooks—germane to the criminal investigation. They mainly involved inexcusably poor liaison with the murdered youth's parents. The Report would have it otherwise. A persistent thread is that the failure of some officers to recognise the attack as 'unequivocally racist' from the start hampered the investigation, and was itself a manifestation of racism. In his evidence to the inquiry Detective Sergeant Davidson accepted that 'one essence' of the attack was racist, but stuck to his view that the suspects would have killed anyone that night:

> because these lads had attacked whites before, very ... similarly with a similar knife. I believe this was thugs. They were described as the Krays. They were thugs who were out to kill, not particu-

larly a black person..., and I believe that to this day that that was thugs, not racism, just pure bloody minded thuggery'.[4]

The Report adds that this was the attitude of as many as 50 per cent of those involved in the investigation.

The notion that racism was one of several mingled motives for the attack on Stephen Lawrence is not self-evidently absurd. Yet the Report finds the attitude of these officers 'deplorable'. Why? Because 'any suggestion that this was not a purely racist murder is understandably anathema to Mr and Mrs Lawrence and indeed to the black community ... and can only lead to the conclusion in the minds of Mr and Mrs Lawrence that proper concentration was not brought to bear upon the investigation of the racist murder of their son, and that such an approach must have skewed the nature and direction of the investigation'.[5]

The Report goes on: 'We consider that their inability to accept that the murder was racist is a manifestation of their own ... unwitting collective racism'.[6] These passages deserve careful pondering.

Third, had the inquiry been genuinely open-minded, I believe it would have used a different explanatory framework. It would have concluded that the main reason for the failure to secure justice for the murdered Stephen Lawrence was gross deficiencies in the police investigation, and that this was all too typical of police handling of low-profile crime. 'Institutional racism' would have been at best a subsidiary theme. But it was appointed to do a political job, and faithfully discharged its brief.

Let me say, in conclusion, that I think there is something in the notion of 'unwitting' racism, hard though it is to pin down. I have been a victim, and perpetrator, of it myself. It lies in making certain assumptions about individuals on the basis of generalised information, or usually misinformation, and is often no more than an awkward attempt to establish contact without knowing what the rules are. The point is, though, that without some tolerance of these 'mistakes' it is hard to know how any relationships between members of different ethnic groups can be established at all.

This brings me to my final criticism of the Report. Nowhere does it begin to consider the possible cost of trying to outlaw 'unwitting racism'—it is even suggested that 'racist language and behaviour' in private places should be subject to prosecution. So fanatic is the Report's determination to stamp out 'unwitting racism' that it is willing to contemplate the imposition of a police state to achieve its aims. For this alone one should condemn the mentality which produced it. It is deeply illiberal in spirit. But the saddest thing of all is that it never begins to consider what effect this, and other recommendations, would have on race relations in this country.

Britain has every reason to be proud of its record in race relations. Taking this Report seriously would carry a real risk of converting unwitting racism into overt racism. The government will, and should, carefully consider which of its recommendations to apply.

Does Institutional Racism Exist In the Metropolitan Police Service?

John G.D. Grieve and Julie French

Introduction

During a recent press conference, Vikram Dodd from *The Guardian* asked if the racism of my colleagues bothered me. I replied that everyone's racism bothered me—including my own— but that I tried to do something about it on a daily basis. This brought a response of both criticism and incredulity. This paper shows what 'trying to do something about it' means to us on a 'daily basis'.[1]

I am a racist. I must be because Sir William Macpherson of Cluny said that I am; the Home Secretary said that I am; countless members of the public at the inquiry hearings said that I am; and I have found inside myself evidence of subtle prejudice, preconception and indirect discrimination. It is for others to decide about their own racism. I am for change inside myself and in the behaviour of myself and others.

The Metropolitan Police Service (MPS) is an institutionally racist organisation. It must be because Sir William Macpherson of Cluny said that it is; the Home Secretary said that it is; countless members of the public at the inquiry hearings said that it is; and we have found inside this organisation evidence of the things spoken about in a poem written by a friend of mine. This is the best statement about racism, overt and covert, indirect and direct,

With special recognition and thanks to John Sutherland and Richard Walton for their considerable contributions.

witting or unwitting, institutional or personal that we have come across in the long months since we took on our roles half-way through the Stephen Lawrence public inquiry.

RACISM

It's In the Way
It's in the way you patronise
The way that you avert your eyes
The way that you cannot disguise
Your looks of horror and surprise

It's the assumptions that you make
On my behalf and for my sake
And in the way you do not hear
The things we tell you loud and clear

It's in the way you touch my hair
The way you think, The way you stare
It's right there in your history
Just like slavery for me

It's in the language that you use
The way that you express your views
The way you always get to choose
The way we lose

It's when you say 'No offence to you'
And then offend me, as you do
It's in your paper policy
Designed by you, for you, not me

It's in the power you abuse
It's on TV, it's in the news
It's in employment, in your school
The way you take me for a fool

It's in the way you change my name
The way that you deny my pain
It's in the way that you collude
To tell me it's my attitude

It's in your false democracy
It's in the chains you cannot see
It's how you talk equality
And then you put it back on me

It's in the way you get annoyed
And say I must be paranoid
It's in the way we have to fight
For basic fundamental human rights

It's in the invasion of my space
It's how you keep me in my place
It's the oppression of my race
IT'S IN MY FACE

Andrea Cork[2]

Institutional racism is more than an academic construct. It is a real experience in the lives of countless Londoners. It is this practical outcome, this reality, that we are seeking to address here, but in order to do so we will first discuss some of the theories about institutional racism.

The Evolving Concept Of Institutional Racism

Racism casts long shadows into the past and the future. Black people have been an integral part of this country's history for over 1,700 years. Most people will be unaware that the first burial of a black person in the United Kingdom was by Hadrian's Wall in approximately 252 AD. Race relations have always been a source of great emotion, so it is very important to understand the concepts and the realities concerned. It is important to be objective and to open up the arguments for third-party analysis and debate.

During the public inquiry we examined three academic approaches to institutional racism:

1. Lord Scarman's Report of the Inquiry into the Brixton Disorders, 1981

2. Dr Robin Oakley's paper 'Institutional Racism and Police Service Delivery'

3. The findings of industrial tribunals.

1. Lord Scarman

It was during Lord Scarman's inquiry into the Brixton Disorders of 1981 that the issues of 'institutional racism' were first discussed in relation to the MPS.

Scarman did not define racism, but concentrated on evidence of 'racial prejudice'. He concerned himself with overt actions and the behaviour of officers who acted out personal prejudices. He stated that:

> Racial prejudice does manifest itself occasionally in the behaviour of a few officers on the streets ... Racially prejudiced behaviour by officers below the level of senior direction of the force is not common; but it does occur, and every instance of it has an immense impact on the community's attitudes and beliefs.[3]

He concluded:

> I find that the direction and policies of the Metropolitan Police Service are not racist. But racial prejudice does manifest itself occasionally in the behaviour of a few officers on the streets.[4]

This view of police racism became more commonly known as the 'bad apple thesis'.[5] A significant issue here is the manifestation of prejudice and Lord Scarman's emphasis of behaviour 'on the streets'.

In respect of the concept of 'institutional racism', Lord Scarman said:

> It was alleged by some of those who made representations to me that Britain is an institutionally racist society. If by that it is meant that it is a society that knowingly, as a matter of policy, discriminates against black people, I reject the allegation. If, however, the suggestion being made is that practices may be adopted by public bodies as well as by private individuals which are unwittingly discriminatory against black people, then this is an allegation which deserves serious consideration, and where proved, swift remedy.[6]

It was, however, with the 'knowingly, as a matter of policy' definition of institutional racism that the MPS began the public inquiry in March 1998. As the inquiry progressed, certain common themes began to emerge in the evidence.

Some of the questioning centred on officers' attitudes and behaviour in relation to racism, racially motivated crime and the definition of racist crime. Their responses highlighted to me a general lack of awareness and understanding. We began to realise that the inquiry panel were eliciting evidence of a form of racism that had not been followed up by us, post Scarman, and that had not yet been fully defined, understood by society or recorded publicly. It could be recognised when it occurred, as Andrea Cork's poem showed me.

We were faced with the challenge of broadening and deepening our understanding of the debate that was evolving in front of us. We were faced with the challenge of changing the experience of the victims of racism.

2. Dr Robin Oakley

Dr Robin Oakley completed a paper entitled 'Institutional Racism and Police Service Delivery' in which he outlined his understanding of racist conduct.

In April 1998 he presented his ideas to the public inquiry and stated that:

> Police work, unlike most other professional activities, has the capacity to bring officers into contact with a skewed cross-section of society with well recognised potential for producing negative stereotypes of particular groups. Such stereotypes become the common currency of the police occupational culture ... failure to address them [negative stereotypes] is liable to result in a generalised tendency, particularly where any element of discretion is involved, whereby minorities may receive different and less favourable treatment than the majority. Such differential treatment need be neither conscious nor intentional and it may be practised routinely by officers whose professionalism is exemplary in all other respects.[7]

Following a series of dialogues with Dr Oakley, some of them quite heated, it became apparent to me just how far the debate regarding institutional racism had progressed since the days of Lord Scarman, and how far many of us had clung to the 'knowingly, as a matter of policy' side of the debate.

Oakley described a form of racism that is:

> Usually covert rather than overt, unintended so far as motivation is concerned, acted out unconsciously by individuals, and an expression of collective rather than purely individual sentiment.

Particularly on account of the latter characteristic, this may be appropriately referred to as a form of 'institutional racism'.[8]

Dr Oakley's description stimulated debate and broadened my team's understanding of the complexities involved.

At this time, there was still no commonly agreed and understood definition of institutional racism. It was therefore understandably problematic for the Commissioner and for all of us to accept the label of 'institutional racism' for the MPS.

3. Industrial Tribunals

Beyond my conversations with Dr Oakley, we looked at the experience of industrial tribunals, where the appeal process has been identified as a means of examining the concept of institutional racism. Three cases in particular further highlighted the complexities we were facing.

King v. Great Britain – China Centre, the Court of Appeal

This upheld an industrial tribunal ruling that it was entitled to draw the inference of discrimination in the presence of an explanation that was seen as inadequate or unsatisfactory. Guidance was given by L.J. Neill, who stated that:

> A finding of discrimination and a finding of a difference in race will often point to the possibility of racial discrimination. In such circumstances the tribunal will look to the employer for an explanation. If no explanation is then put forward or if the tribunal considers the explanation to be inadequate or unsatisfactory it will be legitimate for the tribunal to infer that the discrimination was on racial grounds.[9]

E.A.T Chattopadhyay v. Headmaster of Holloway School and Others

It was held that:

> Since it is rare for an applicant complaining of discrimination to have evidence of overtly racial discriminatory words or actions, he had to rely on facts, which, if unexplained, were consistent with

him having been treated less favourably than others on racial grounds. In the majority of cases it is only the respondent and their witnesses who are able to say whether in fact the allegedly discriminatory act was motivated by racial discrimination or by other, perfectly innocent motivations. It is for this reason that the law has been established that if an applicant shows that he has been treated less favourably than others in circumstances which are consistent with that treatment being based on racial grounds, the industrial tribunal should draw an inference that such treatment was on racial grounds, unless the respondent can satisfy the industrial tribunal that there is an innocent explanation.[10]

Qureshi v. London Borough of Newham

It was held that:

> Incompetence does not, without more, become discrimination because the person affected by it is from an ethnic minority.[11]

All three of these approaches to racial prejudice have validity. During the Stephen Lawrence inquiry, there was an absence of evidence of express racism but it became apparent that a form of racism was being displayed by officers. This emerged through the catalogue of errors revealed during the initial investigation into the murder of Stephen Lawrence and subsequently through the evidence given by officers during the public inquiry.

When the Commissioner and I attended Part II of the public inquiry on Wednesday 1 October 1998, he did not accept that the MPS was institutionally racist. Most significantly, he would not accept that the MPS is racist 'knowingly, as a matter of policy'. The inquiry panel did not at that time produce a definition of institutional racism.

The weekend before the findings were published brought detailed leaks that were personally and organisationally devastating. On 24 February 1999, the Stephen Lawrence inquiry report provided the definition as determined by Sir William Macpherson of Cluny, *viz.*:

> The collective failure of an organisation to provide an appropriate and professional service to people because of their colour, culture, or ethnic origin. It can be seen or detected in processes, attitudes and behaviour which amount to discrimination through unwitting prejudice, ignorance, thoughtlessness and racist stereotyping which disadvantage minority ethnic people.[12]

The definition showed some clear similarities with Scarman's observations concerning 'unwitting racism' and, more recently, Dr Oakley's analysis of 'covert' rather than 'overt' racism. Sir William Macpherson concluded that institutional racism, within the terms of the definition:

> exists both in the Metropolitan Police Service and other services and other institutions countrywide.[13]

This definition provided the clarity that we had sought and we accepted that the police service is institutionally racist within these parameters.

Accepting this 'label' has been a painful process and indeed, the months following this acceptance have proved to be extraordinarily challenging for our organisation. The one thing I can find to be proud of looking back is that we never hid behind the racism of 'other services' or 'institutions countrywide'.

So What Does Institutional Racism Mean To Me?

Having explored some of the debate I now want to examine what institutional racism means to me at a personal level.

> As I watched her walk towards her car I wondered if I too had fallen prey to that old white pretence of impatient charity with people of colour as if they were somehow incapable of understanding our efforts on their behalf.[14]

Institutional racism is about stereotyping; it is about being unwitting; it is about ignorance; it is about failing to recognise a racist/hate crime; it is about not listening or understanding and not being interested in listening or understanding; it is about white pretence and black people being seen as a problem.

I have a clear recollection of racism at home, work, church, school and during my career as a police officer within the MPS. The last eighteen months have been difficult but enlightening. Working together with representatives from the diverse communities of London, I have been privileged to participate in a fundamental process of change.

We have all come a long way and I know of no other organisation that could have been as flexible as the MPS and adapted so quickly. We have faced up to our responsibilities and tackled these challenges head on. What we have seen is a paradigm shift in social awareness and the police are in the forefront of this response. That does not mean, of course, that experiences of all victims are satisfactory.

What Have I Done About It?

The way that we police London has changed significantly and it will continue to do so as we enter the twenty-first century. We must continue to evolve as an organisation in order to meet the diverse needs of the communities we serve. That process of change has already begun.

In November 1998 the MPS launched its Diversity Strategy ('Protect and Respect'). This established the organisational commitment to develop an anti-racist police service, to improve the recruitment and advancement of minority ethnic officers, to improve the transparency and accountability of the organisation and to improve the investigation and prevention of racist crime.

Prior to this, in August 1998, the Racial and Violent Crime Task Force (RVCTF) was established and I was appointed Director. We developed an action plan to combat racist/hate crime.

The first thing to discover was the experience on the streets. The Intelligence Cell Analysis System (ICAS) was established to provide a clearer and more focused picture of racist and hate crime in the capital. It has become an integral part of the RVCTF. ICAS is staffed by forward-thinking strategic and tactical analysts with innovative intelligence officers and who report directly to me. It is also a by-word for open source, publicly available and shared intelligence with the very street agencies who gave such powerful evidence against us to Sir William.

It has become a pilot site for pioneering intelligence research tools, including databases that provide simultaneous data capture extending over eighty intelligence databases. ICAS has developed in order to progress reactive investigations, proactive intelligence-led operations and medium- to long-term intelligence initiatives.

I suggest that the MPS Independent Advisory Group, established in January 1999, has been the source of the most fundamental changes to affect the organisation. When I invited some of our sternest critics, some of whom had given evidence to Sir William, into the MPS to review our processes and procedures and to advise on how we could become an anti-racist police service, I knew that it was not going to be easy. Famously, one of them said 'we are not nodding dogs'. This process will now form a fundamental component of twenty-first century policing.

The blueprint for corporate lay-involvement includes the effective intervention of lay advisors in operational policing, their strategic intervention in the MPS Diversity Programme and the definition of options for the future police operating environment in support of the Metropolitan Police Authority. This will ensure that the MPS is both accountable and transparent.

In June 1999 Community Safety Units were launched in every London borough to provide a corporate focus for the investigation and prevention of racist/hate crime and domestic violence.

Within the Stephen Lawrence report, family liaison and victim care feature significantly. Mr and Mrs Lawrence were let down by the MPS due to a lack of structures, training and understanding of victim and family care. We conducted research nationally to establish if other constabularies had already addressed this obvious area of development. Avon and Somerset Constabulary had in place an extensive six-day course that covers all facets of family liaison.

Since November 1998, the RVCTF has facilitated training of family liaison officers through Avon and Somerset Constabulary. A central database is held by our unit to assist in the management of the cadre. My ambition is for the role of the family liaison officer to be equal to that of a hostage negotiator and firearms officers, where specialist skills are recognised, supported and progressed by the organisation.

Within eighteen months of the creation of the RVCTF, there had been a 900 per cent increase in racist/hate intelligence and arrests and reporting increased by over 250 per cent.

Some Of The Wider Issues

Sir William Macpherson of Cluny made it very clear in his report that institutional racism is not unique to the police. We are facing challenges that must also be faced by society as a whole.

In October 1999, staff at Ford's Dagenham plant held a strike ballot after a multi-racial walk out in protest at racist attitudes apparently held by some management and the denial of equal opportunities for promotion:

> About 45 per cent of workers at Dagenham are from ethnic minorities (a plus point for Ford's race policies), but only a very small proportion of senior or managerial jobs go to them.[15]

In July 1999, Northern General Hospital Sheffield accepted kidneys for transplantation from a donor who insisted that the recipient should be white. The hospital have said: 'Under no circumstances can we condone the acceptance of organs where there are conditions attached'.

Paul Barker, senior fellow of the Institute of Community Studies, observed that:

> the canker of racism can lie at the heart of even the most benevolent institutions.[16]

Dr George Carey, the Archbishop of Canterbury, has admitted that the church as an institution is guilty of racism.[17] People wanting to join the Church of England will be asked to state their ethnic origin after a plea by Asian and black members of the General Synod to combat 'institutional racism'. Worshippers joining a parish electoral roll will be required to state their ethnic group in an anonymous attachment to the electoral roll form.

There is one Asian diocesan bishop, the Right Reverend Michael Nazir-Ali of Rochester, and two black suffragen bishops, the Right Reverend John Sentamu of Stepney and the Right Reverend Wilfred Wood of Croydon.

As an organisation, the MPS has moved at a tremendous pace, and we still have a long way to go. The real test will be the impact on our service delivery.

In the immediate aftermath of the Stephen Lawrence report the words of Roy Hattersley highlighted the problems that society is facing:

> Ten years ago I had lunch with an Indian millionaire who, it was hoped, would give money to the Labour Party. He said that the big difference between rags and riches was that when he was poor the police stopped him, because they were suspicious of Asians in elderly Fords. When he became rich they stopped him because they were suspicious of Asians in new Mercedes.

He went on to say that:

> Charitably, he described their behaviour as 'innocent', meaning that they honestly thought that they were only doing their duty, and would resent any suggestion of racial bias. They were, he said, men and women who would happily live next door to a black family in the genuine belief that their friendly, law-abiding neighbours were not typical of their race. The real problem, he judged, is that institutional racists have no idea how racist they are.[18]

Another friend of mine, Gus John, Professor at Strathclyde, once said to me:

Your problem, John, is that you think black people are a problem. Black people are not a problem. Stop and search, that's a problem, deaths in custody, that's a problem, street robbery, that's a problem, your son going out and never coming home, that's a problem. Black people are just people. Saying they are a problem is pathological.

Conclusion

Paul Wilson, chair of the newly established National Black Police Association, has very publicly aired his own concerns about the change that the MPS is effecting. In a recent article he highlighted that:

> Quite simply, the perpetuation of institutional racism is reliant upon the dominant ethnic group in any institution preserving their power base. Therefore, the dismantling of institutional racism is reliant upon the dominant ethnic group either voluntarily relinquishing some of that power, or being coerced or compelled to do so.[19]

That is what lay advice, family liaison, open source intelligence and community safety units are trying to achieve.

In Britain after Stephen Lawrence, every individual and institution has a responsibility to examine their behaviour, perception and prejudices. The defence of unwitting racism is closed. As a member of my Independent Advisory Group explained: 'Passive non-racism is no longer acceptable'. For the Met this is a time of profound change. We have made terrible mistakes and my determination is that, in working more closely than ever before with the communities we serve, we seek to build a police service ready to face the challenges of the new millennium—a millennium that is hostile to racists.

Less Race, Please

Michael Ignatieff

For days no one could talk of anything else. The papers were full of editorials saying 'Never again'. The Lawrence inquiry was, we were told, a turning point in attitudes towards race in Britain. Now everything has gone quiet. The cuttings are already yellowing. William Macpherson, chairman of the inquiry, has returned to his castle in Scotland. Mr and Mrs Lawrence have gone their separate ways. Stephen Lawrence's killers are still free.

As with the Scarman report after Brixton, we seem unable to come to any awareness of these issues without a convulsion of guilt-ridden confusion. What is most dismaying, looking back on Lawrence, is that it became a story about just one thing—race. But the central issue was not race, it was justice. Why were we talking about institutionalised racism, when the issue was institutionalised incompetence? Why were we talking about 'race awareness,' when the issue was equal justice before the law?

Everyone talked as if the Lawrence family and a larger fiction called 'the black community' had been 'let down'. The 'black community' is no more of a reality than the 'white community'. To suppose this is to believe that skin trumps all other identities, that we are only our surfaces. In reality the Lawrence family were denied justice, and because they were denied justice, all of us have good reason to feel anger and shame that we cared so little about institutions which operate in our name.

This chapter first appeared in *Prospect* (www.prospect-magazine.co.uk), April 1999, and is reproduced by kind permission.

Looking forward, justice is what is needed, not race awareness training. Blacks and whites surely want to live in a society less aware of race, not more. What conceivable good is served by Macpherson's definition of a 'racist' incident? He says it is 'any incident which is perceived to be racist by the victim or any other person'.[1] If racism is in the eye of the beholder, we will never be finished with it. The Macpherson definition will 'racialise' every encounter between the police and the non-white public to the benefit of neither, while the white public, often badly treated by the police too, will feel that they have no recourse for the indignities they suffer—and will resent the perceived 'positive discrimination' towards non-whites.

Do we seriously suppose that only black people face injustice at the hand of the police? Are we so naïve as to forget that class can count just as much as race in denying people equal protection? Again, there is no way around the simple injunction: all persons, whether rich or poor, black or white, are entitled to the full protection of the law.

I see no useful purpose in trying to change the class or racial attitudes of ordinary policemen. I see every reason to insist, on pain of dismissal, that they understand the meaning of justice. A police recruit needs to understand that the morality of law enforcement turns on the idea of citizenship, not on the idea of group identity. This isn't complicated. It doesn't require advanced sophistication, compassion or understanding, merely the simple awareness that the purpose of the police is to provide equal protection under the law.

To the degree that the police treat people as individuals, their personal opinions about the religion, dietary habits or sexual orientations of the citizens they deal with are strictly irrelevant. They will rightly object to attempts to change their personal opinions. In reality, all they need to change is their behaviour on the beat.

Training the police is a matter of training them to treat people as individuals, and not as genders, races or classes. The point is to make them less 'sensitive', less aware of difference, and more aware of one single identity: that the people they police are their equals, with rights and recourse.

Are we so balkanised into our racial and other group identities that we cannot see this? Commentators talked about their shame, as if it was appropriate for white people to feel shame at what was done to a member of the black community. The shame is for what happened to a fellow citizen, at the hands of a police force supposed to be accountable to us all.

We need a dose of liberal realism. Borrowing from Isaiah Berlin, let us distinguish between positive and negative tolerance. Negative tolerance is the minimum we require in a liberal society. It means protecting minorities from abuse and attack, it means equal treatment by public agencies, level playing fields for employment and so on. But we do not need to love each other, reach out to each other, or even particularly value our different cultures. A minority will practice such positive tolerance and, as time passes, that minority may become a majority. But for now most of us do *not* live together. We live in the same neighbourhoods, watch the same television programmes and visit the same shops, but the various class and ethnic groups often inhabit unfathomably different universes.

What is desperately needed, and is still a generation away, is a happy indifference towards those collective identities and a genuine conviction that the differences that matter most are those between individuals. We do not need to police each other's thoughts and attitudes towards our differences. We simply need to master violence, to punish the kind of attack that occurred at that bus stop in south London, with all the determination that we can muster. And insist—before another courageous mother has to remind us—that justice is indivisible.

The Macpherson Report and Institutional Racism

Mike O'Brien

In 1997 the Prime Minister challenged Britain not just to be a success as a multi-racial society but to be a beacon to the world as a successful multi-racial society. The report of the Stephen Lawrence case indicated just how tough that challenge would be but the Government is determined to deliver on it.

The Lawrence report, with its 70 wide-ranging recommendations, was a watershed for race issues in Britain. It confronted many white people, who had suspected that concerns about racism were exaggerated, with the serious problems that can face ethnic minority people in Britain. It showed that racism manifests itself not just in the vicious attacks by people like the gang of white racist thugs alleged to have killed Stephen Lawrence, but also in the less obvious ways, such as the apparent suspicion and lack of understanding which followed Stephen's stabbing.

The police took the brunt of the criticism, particularly the allegations of institutional racism, but the lesson of the Report is not just about the need to improve our criminal justice system: it has a wider importance. The Report is about securing the commitment of all of us to tackling racism, whether open or unwitting throughout our society, not just in the police force. In responding to Macpherson, the Government is exhibiting clear leadership in tackling race issues. We must all recognise the moral and economic sense in not wasting the talents and abilities of the seven per cent of people who live in Britain and form our ethnic minorities. The Report tells us that racism by individuals and institutions damages our broader society as well as diminishing each of us.

Racism As 'Un-British'

The important thing for all of us is that Britain *is* a multi-racial society. We have a choice whether to succeed as one or not. Racism in all its guises endangers and undermines the future success of our society; that is why to be racist in today's multi-racial Britain is to be 'un-British'.

To be 'British' is not to adopt some narrow cultural norm but to embrace a culture which is increasingly more open, vibrant and enjoys its diversity. A successful multi-racial society must go beyond mere tolerance and embrace this diversity and the benefits that stem from it. After all, we only tolerate what we do not like and in reality, from curry to Reggae, most of us like the benefits of diversity because it makes our country a richer place to be. Indeed, it is not just our minority ethnic communities that have influenced Britain. Culture is becoming much more international, courtesy of the media and the Internet. In some ways we are all in the process of re-defining an image of ourselves as part of a British culture which is wider. It embraces not just multi-culturalism and aspects of international culture but also the 'multi-nationalist' ability to be Welsh, Scottish, English or Northern Irish and British too. As well, perhaps, as being a European citizen.

The 1950's version of Britain remembered by John Major involved warm beer, cricket on the village green and nuns cycling to church on Sunday. Today's culture, particularly among our young people, is less conformist, more an expression of individuality, and is more open to global influences. That fits in well with an image of ourselves as a successful, multi-cultural society. It fits with the history of these islands and our ability over time to adapt and absorb new influences. There is still a recognisable British culture but it has changed in the last 40 years and on balance is better for the changes. The new wider culture enables our ethnic minorities to keep much of their heritage without challenging the social cohesion of our country. The Race Relations Act had undeniably an important role in changing public attitudes. The 1976 Act set a minimum standard for public speech and behaviour which has over time made open racist remarks and behaviour less acceptable. But there is no room for complacency, as the Lawrence case showed. Our society has come a long way, but has a long way to go to achieve race equality.

Of course, any change on this scale produces insecurity among those who have difficulty adapting to it. This can result in a search for scapegoats.

The increasing numbers of recorded racial incidents may well reflect a greater willingness to report this type of incident, helped by better statistical reporting and a clearer definition following the Macpherson inquiry. It is also possible that there has been some increase in the number of racial incidents themselves. Social deviancy manifesting itself as racial hatred may not be easy to eradicate, even as the numbers practising it decline.

The Government is committed to tough laws to tackle racist crimes. The Crime and Disorder Act 1998 introduced nine new offences which require stiffer sentences where there is a racial motivation in respect of a crime of racial harassment or violence. These harsher sentences reflect society's particular abhorrence of racial crime, because it so undermines the social fabric of Britain. The new laws are important. So too is the new Race Relations (Amendment) Bill, which will extend the Race Relations Act to the police and the rest of the public sector. The new law will create a duty on all public authorities to promote equality of opportunity and good relations between persons of different racial groups. This means that the state and public organisations receiving taxpayers' money will be part of the process of making Britain a more equal society. Every public authority will have to put in place the means of ensuring that their internal organisation is fair to ethnic minorities and that in the delivery of their services they pay attention to race issues. The law will be on the side of tackling race inequality in institutions.

Institutional Racism

Britain cannot become a successful multi-racial society unless it tackles race equality issues and ensures that we give people from ethnic minority communities a fair chance to succeed on merit. Tackling inequality in an organisation requires an acceptance that there is a problem to be addressed in the first place.

Some deny there is any problem in their organisation. They point out with some truth that Britain has changed in the last 40 years. Racism is increasingly frowned upon in the business community and in polite society. There is also a strong and growing black and Asian middle class. Most organisations want to recruit the most able people irrespective of race, and so they want to treat everyone fairly.

All this is true but it ignores other facts. There are other forms of inequality which deny fairness to people. They disadvantage one group as against another in a way which ignores merit. Unemployment rates among ethnic minority people, for example, are higher than for white people regardless of qualification, age, gender or location. Overall, people from ethnic minority communities are as well qualified as white people, but that is not reflected in managerial and senior positions held by them in organisations. Their average income tends to be lower and they are more likely to live in deprived areas, in overcrowded housing and to be disproportionately excluded from better quality schools and access to other social goods. This is an issue which needs to be addressed in our society as a whole and within our organisations.

The concept of institutional racism has been used for some time to describe unjustifiable ethnic minority disadvantage within organisations. It recognises that an organisation may not intend to act in a racist way, but that its structures or its culture means that patterns of recruitment, promotion or service delivery may result in people from racial minorities being disadvantaged. It is a challenging concept which has produced a good deal of controversy.

Today, it is pejorative to be called a racist. No-one with sense wants to be associated with racism. Nor do they want the organisation which they work for to be regarded as racist. Having won the debate that to be racist is morally repugnant, many advocates of race equality have sought to go beyond that and get people to accept that they should label their own organisation as institutionally racist. Not surprisingly, some people find it difficult to accept. It makes us feel uncomfortable whether we are white or black—but then, maybe we need to feel uncomfortable about this issue.

The debate appeared to be largely academic in tone until the Lawrence report thrust it into the centre of public debate. The report asked, not only whether the police were racist, but whether they were institutionally racist?

The Lawrence report defined institutional racism as 'the collective failure of an organisation to provide an appropriate and professional service to people because of their colour, culture, or ethnic origin. It can be seen or detected in processes, attitudes and behaviour which amount to discrimination through unwitting prejudice, ignorance, thoughtlessness and racist stereotyping which disadvantage minority ethnic people'. The report went on to say that institutional racism 'persists because of the failure of the organisation openly and adequately to recognise and address its existence and causes by policy, example and leadership. Without recognition and action to eliminate such racism it can prevail as part of the ethos or culture of the organisation'.

The use of the phrase 'unwitting' in the Stephen Lawrence Report allowed people to accept that there had been unintended disadvantage to ethnic minorities. The Metropolitan Police accepted the definition and set out on a programme of institutional change. They drafted in one of their most able officers to lead the transformation, John Grieve, the former head of the anti-terrorist squad. He set about the task with skill and courage.

Some organisations, like the Church of England and the TUC, also examined how to tackle institutional racism within their own organisations. Jack Straw, the Home Secretary, accepted the definition and set about making the Home Office into a model of equality-focused transformations. But only a few other organisations accepted the label.

It not only made people uncomfortable, it also remained little understood by many. They believed their organisation was not intentionally racist because they abhorred racism, so were uncomfortable with the word 'racism' in the new definition. As the definition allowed for 'unwitting' prejudice, ignorance, thoughtlessness and racist stereotyping of people they were also unsure quite what they were admitting when they signed up to it.

Regrettably, the fight for a broad acceptance of the label has also become handicapped by the impression that if someone says that their organisation is institutionally racist, that it discredits everything the organisation does because it might be inspired by racist sentiments, even if the organisation is determinedly following anti-racist policies.

The programme of organisational change within the Home Office will create equal opportunities for everyone. Yet when there was an acceptance of institutional racism, the Home Office and its policies were condemned as tainted by racism. It did not encourage others to embrace the concept for their organisation.

This is regrettable as institutional racism is a valuable concept. The Lawrence report suggested that accepting it is the first step to tackling equality and transforming an organisation. The concept is therefore an important one which we should support.

In some cases the reluctance of organisations is not so much to accept the problem or to implement programmes to effect change, it is rather to accept the label.

Other labels have been accepted more easily. Whilst people accept working for an 'equal opportunities employer' because it has a positive ring, some do not want to openly embrace a label which requires an admission of 'collective failure' of an organisation, no matter how valid or worthy it is.

This presents a dilemma. Do we retreat from a challenging concept and apt phrase because it is uncomfortable? Or do we maintain the label but allow the reluctance to accept it to interfere with the implementation of practical programmes to tackle racial disadvantage within organisations? Could we strengthen the equality agenda faster if we toned down the language?

A Theory Of Transformation

The concept of institutional racism is most helpful as a description of an organisation which has yet to become conscious of race issues within its culture or has suffered a serious breakdown in its consciousness. However, there is a qualitative difference between an organisation which has never recognised problems of race inequality, or is conscious of them but has failed to address them, compared to one which is seriously and actively transforming itself to create race equality.

Of course institutional racism does not evaporate merely by recognising it within the organisation and trying to change its culture, but once sustainable change is under way then the nature of the organisation is different and the concept and the label should recognise that.

We must not retreat from the valuable work done by Macpherson in defining institutional racism and demanding that steps be taken to address it, rather it needs to be built upon by creating a new body of language and theory which describes a process of change and transformation. I suggest that Macpherson's definition does describe an organisation which has yet to put in place policies to address race but it may not fully describe an organisation in transition, nor one which has made substantial progress on race equality.

The Race Relations (Amendment) Bill when enacted will place a general duty on all public authorities to promote race equality. The general duty will be supplemented by specific duties which will also be prescribed in regulations and enforceable by the Commission on Racial Equality (CRE). The CRE will be empowered to issue Codes of Practice. These will be subject to public consultation, the approval of the Secretary of State and Parliament. Existing CRE Codes of Practice for local authorities set standards for organisations to achieve. As organisations demonstrate progress in race equality, they move up to the next level against those standards. Progress can, therefore, be measured over time and organisations can take pride in or be embarrassed by their ranking.

Some organisations are addressing race in a rigorous way. The language needs to be flexible enough to describe the process or the stage of it which they have reached.

There is a real challenge to academics to link the substantial body of work on the managerial theory of organisational change to the wider research that has been carried out on race equality. We can build on the foundations of the Lawrence report to develop language and theory which can help articulate the transition from institutional racism to race equality and which can give confidence to people that they are on the side of helping to make Britain a successful multi-racial society.

Creating A Race Equality Organisation

As stated before, the new Race Relations (Amendment) Bill will place a positive duty on public authorities. These new laws will provide impetus for change in our public institutions, including their internal managerial policies. The Home Office is the lead department in Whitehall on tackling race inequality. A staff survey in 1997 for the Home Office revealed that a disappointing 40 per cent of ethnic minority staff felt that they had been disadvantaged or discriminated against. It suggested we were not attracting sufficient numbers of the best and brightest people from ethnic minorities because our organisation was not giving them enough encouragement.

As a result of this, the Home Office, led by Jack Straw and the Permanent Secretary, David Omand, set in motion a programme of widespread change which addresses issues around institutional racism and has been seen in Whitehall as a model for building a 'race equality organisation'.

One important step is that the Home Secretary has already set targets for the recruitment, retention and promotion of ethnic minorities within the Home Office and all its services, including the police, the fire service and the prison service. That is not to say that the problem is apparent throughout the Home Office and its services—indeed some parts of the organisation recruit well. The Immigration and Nationality Directorate has 20 per cent ethnic minority staff. This compares with the fire service which has less than two per cent. However, in senior grades across the Home Office the proportion of black and Asian people falls to below two per cent. The aim is to get overall recruitment to the national average for ethnic minorities at about seven per cent, and to have local targets where ethnic minorities are a higher percentage of the population, such as in London. The targets are set for implementation over ten years with milestones along the way. They seek to address not only the initial recruitment but also the retention and valuing of able black and Asian people and to ensure that barriers to their promotion are removed.

Importantly, these are targets not quotas. Quotas are illegal and are opposed by most of the minority ethnic communities. People are not looking for privileges or favouritism, merely an equal chance. Targets are about fairness, rewarding talent and putting an end to glass ceilings. Managers will have to deliver the targets or justify not hitting them in the same way as any other management target. They will be judged on their ability to deliver.

These targets are necessary because evidence shows that ethnic minorities often do not get a fair deal, particularly on promotion. Jack Straw uses the example of Asian women. Often white men hear about a possible job in the pub after work and it is there that they receive encouragement to apply for it from their managers. Asian women rarely go to the pub after work. They do not know about the job and are not encouraged to apply for it. To assist managers to prevent this problem, in the Home Office an ethnic minority network has been set up to provide mutual support and encouragement to staff. It is part of our broad-based approach to enabling ethnic minority staff to play their full part in the organisation. The network has top management commitment and the full support of ministers. Top management and senior officials are also taking on the role of mentoring able staff from ethnic minorities to encourage their progress in the organisation. The Home Secretary is determined that the Home Office and its services will be a beacon of good practice to other parts of the public sector.

Positive progress within the Home Office should pave the way for the introduction of similar targets in all Whitehall departments and public sector organisations and we hope in due course that the private sector will decide itself to adopt them.

As part of the civil service reform programme each department has to assess where it is on the diversity spectrum and state what it aims to do in order to improve. The Home Office has made progress but there is more work to be done.

Internal management reform, committed leadership and local role models are important but we must also remember that we must improve the output and quality of service that is delivered to ethnic minorities if we are to address institutional racism.

The new duty to promote race equality will also oblige public authorities to integrate race equality into policy making, implementation and service delivery and not, as often in the past, regard it as a simple add-on. It will underpin a policy adopted by the Home Office and other government departments, for example, commonly known as mainstreaming. It will mean that, when considering any policy or managerial change, ministers and managers should explicitly consider the impact on race equality. The implementation of public policies which achieve race equality will play a major part in the drive towards making race equality a reality and towards building communities with confidence in their public services, including the police, whether as employees or customers.

It is here that the Home Secretary's Race Relations Forum has a key role. This forum was set up in 1997 in order to bring in people from ethnic minorities to advise the government on aspects of policy. We are making full use of the knowledge and experience of forum members, who come from different backgrounds, to develop our strategic thinking on the ways of implementing our policies and measuring progress.

Measuring progress in race equality will be important. We have therefore been working to develop a basket of indicators of service delivery that will measure improvements in race equality across key areas of government activity. We will then be able to have comparative data to measure the impact of government services and broader policy on ethnic minority communities, compared with the majority of the community.

Britain as a country has come a long way in the last 40 years. What was acceptable in language, behaviour and public discourse in those days is no longer tolerated. There are still those who seek to reverse the process, the sort of people who tend to describe using language which shows respect for others as mere 'political correctness'. Such people are trying to find a label to justify bad manners and disrespect for others. But by and large our society has changed for the better. We need to recognise that and encourage the process of change. We must pick up the pace and continue with the process. Change may be difficult in the short term but in the long term it will make us stronger and more successful. After all, tackling racism is not just about helping ethnic minorities. We are all part of a multi-racial society and we succeed or fail together.

The truth is we cannot afford to fail. If we do, our children will pay a high price. If we succeed we all benefit. That is why it is important that we get the language, the theory and the practical policies right.

Commentary

Racial Preferences Are Not the Best Way to Create Racial Harmony

David G. Green

What is the best way to create racial harmony? The traditional liberal ideal was stated clearly in Martin Luther King's famous 'I Have a Dream' speech, delivered in August 1963 in Washington, DC:

> I have a dream that my four little children will one day live in a nation where they will not be judged by the colour of their skin but by the content of their character.

When applied to policing this ideal means that individuals should be equal before the law and judged only according to their actual behaviour. From the earliest days of policing this ideal of equal treatment under the law was clearly understood. In 1829 guiding principles for the newly-formed Metropolitan Police Force said:

> The police seek and preserve public favour, not by catering to public opinion, but by constantly demonstrating absolute impartial service to the law, in complete independence of policy, and without regard to the justice or injustice of the substance of individual laws; by ready offering of individual service and friendship to all members of society without regard to their race or social standing.[1]

In recent times there has been a weakening of the ideal that the police and the courts should be 'colour blind' in precisely the manner that justice is said to be blind. When the Macpherson report accused the Metropolitan Police Service of 'institutional racism', it led the police to reject

37

their earlier belief in colour blind policing. The courts have also been affected. A booklet produced by the Equal Treatment Advisory Committee for the Judicial Studies Board, the official agency for advising judges, begins with the statement that: 'Justice in a modern and diverse society must be "colour conscious", not "colour blind".' And in order to emphasise the point, a list of nine 'dos and don'ts' includes: 'Be "colour conscious" not "colour blind".'[2]

We can understand these developments better by considering them in the wider international context brilliantly described by the black American economist, Thomas Sowell. He suggests that we understand campaigns for racial preferences as one among several strategies to become a *government*-designated group which benefits from *government*-mandated preferences.[3] The chapter by the Home Office Minister, Mike O'Brien, describes how the Government intends to impose on all public authorities a policy of 'race equality'. The Home Office has taken the lead and introduced targets which assume that because ethnic groups comprise seven per cent of the total UK population they should comprise seven per cent of the police, the fire service and the civil service, including senior grades. Mr O'Brien denies that they are quotas and insists they are only 'targets', but if they constrain the behaviour of managers making appointments there is, at the very least, a resemblance to quotas. Either way, this policy is a departure from the ideal of recruitment solely according to the ability of candidates to do the job.

Many rationales for preferential treatment have been deployed, but here we are concerned with groups who base their appeal on race, whether they are minorities or majorities. According to Sowell, in various countries throughout the world groups calling for racial preferences have used four main grounds: racial superiority; the rights of indigenous peoples; the need to compensate for historic wrongs; and 'disproportionate representation' in sections of society, such as desirable occupations.

Racial superiority was claimed in the Deep South of the USA, Nazi Germany and South Africa. The rights of indigenous peoples have been asserted by the Malays over Chinese immigrants to Malaysia, by black Ugandans against Asian Ugandans, and most recently by native Fijians against Fijian Asians. Historical wrongs have been asserted by the Chinese in Malaysia, American Indians and Aboriginals in Australia. Disproportionate representation is the newest of the strategies for racial preference, and has been successfully deployed by black Americans. It is the strategy favoured by some leaders of ethnic minorities in Britain.

The underlying assumption is that the ratio of one racial group to another in the total population should be reflected in every sub-group. Thus, if ethnic minorities comprise ten per cent of the total population, they should make up ten per cent of every occupational group, such as teachers, lawyers or doctors, including ten per cent at every level of seniority. If there is a disparity, the cause is assumed to be 'discrimination', and if anyone points out that there could be other causes, such as a lack of aptitude or qualifications or even simple personal preferences, they are accused of 'blaming the victim'. As Sowell writes:

> By making the issue, *who* is to blame, such arguments evade or pre-empt the more fundamental question—whether this is a matter of blame in the first place.[4]

In other words, this line of reasoning confuses causation with blame. To explain a cause is not to attribute blame, but merely to try to understand the reasons for an outcome.

For example, some ethnic groups will be *over*-represented in some occupations out of choice. Many of the first generation to arrive in the UK from India, for example, chose to run small shops, not least because such businesses permit the whole family to play an active part in contributing to the family's advance. Shopkeepers cannot simultaneously be doctors or lawyers, leading to *under-*

representation in those occupations. None of this is to argue that there is no racism at all in Britain. We have all encountered individuals who are prejudiced, and it hardly needs to be said that if racism leads to criminal actions against ethnic minorities the perpetrators should not be allowed to get away with it. However, if the incompetence of a public service has a disparate impact on one ethnic group compared with another, or if there is disproportionate representation in occupations, it cannot automatically be assumed that prejudice is either the sole, or even a contributing, cause.

To sum up: we can best understand the debate about proportionate representation for ethnic minorities as an aspect of a racial strategy by a group, or its self-appointed champions, to gain political recognition for its 'victim' status in order to demand preferential policies as compensation for alleged discrimination. It is a strategy which can only work in a society made up largely of fair-minded people who are anxious to make all its members feel at home, regardless of their ethnic origin. Essentially, it is a strategy for exploiting their good intentions.

It is probably still too soon to look back on the murder of Stephen Lawrence and the Macpherson inquiry with a wholly dispassionate eye, but I predict that when impartial observers can finally look upon these events with the cooler perspective of time it will be possible to see more clearly that the tragic murder of a young man and the distress of his bereaved parents has been exploited by pressure groups intent on establishing credibility for their claim that black people in Britain are victims who should be given preferential treatment. Their intention has been to demonstrate that 'white' society did not care about the death of a black man. But, as Norman Dennis, Ahmed Al-Shahi and George Erdos show in their companion volume, *Racist Murder and Pressure-Group Politics*, no evidence was found to justify any such claim, even by the Macpherson inquiry, whose methods at times were more like a kangaroo court than a judicial process. Indeed, far from being unconcerned about the murder of a black person, the first white people (Mr and Mrs Taaffe) to encounter Stephen Lawrence after the stabbing showed kindness and concern. After doing her best to ensure that he was in the 'recovery position', Mrs Taaffe had touched Stephen's head and comforted him with the words, 'You are loved, you are loved'. And after they returned home, Mr Taaffe washed Stephen's blood from his hands and poured the water containing it at the foot of a rose tree, in Stephen's memory. The Macpherson report said that their actions deserved 'nothing but praise' and were 'to be applauded'.[5]

The real lesson of the police investigation is not that the police did not care about the murder; it is that they were bad at their job. This revelation of police incompetence and mishandling in reality gave all Londoners, black or white, something in common: a shared concern to improve the police service for the good of all. Instead, the episode has increased racial polarisation.

Sowell's identification of the four main strategies deployed by, or on behalf of, racial groups to secure preferences enables us to see that they all have in common the pursuit of group self-interest at the expense of another group. The typical consequence everywhere has been to increase group selfishness and group resentment, a trend which is incompatible with the ideal of a free society built on equality before the law.

Sowell has also shown that there have typically been some other unexpected consequences of preferential policies based on race. For example, within the groups politically designated as entitled to preferences, the benefits have usually gone disproportionately to those who are already most fortunate. This should not be particularly surprising since the chief advocates of preferential policies are intellectuals who tend to define grievances in terms of their own unmet aspirations. The rationale for group preferences is that the 'less fortunate' members of society

watchwords. By contrast, the closing line of the poem, 'It's in my face', is an assertion of aggressive self-absorption.

The Macpherson report was a watershed in British race relations and has led to the adoption of policies which are likely to diminish rather than improve racial harmony. The fundamental danger is that, in our efforts to ensure that everyone within our frontiers feels at home, we fall prey to the subtle arguments of groups demanding racial preferences. A free and democratic society depends first and foremost on equality before the law and it relies on the sense of solidarity we all feel because we agree to live under common rules which, by restraining us in certain agreed respects, release the potential of everyone to make the most of his or her talents. Such solidarity is a far better safeguard for good community relations than policies of racial preference.

Appendix

The following set of principles, which lay out in the clearest and most succinct terms the philosophy of policing by consent, appeared as an appendix to *A New Study of Police History* by Charles Reith (London: Oliver and Boyd, 1956). Reith was a lifelong historian of the police force in Britain, and this book covers the early years of Metropolitan Police following the passage of Sir Robert Peel's 'Bill for Improving the Police in and near the Metropolis' on 19 June 1829. Reith notes that there are particular problems involved in writing police history, owing to the loss or destruction of much early archive material, and, probably for this reason, the principles appear without details of author or date. However, it seems most likely that they were composed by Charles Rowan and Richard Mayne, as the first and joint Commissioners of the Metropolitan Police. Rowan was a military man and Mayne, fourteen years his junior, a barrister. Rowan retired in 1850 leaving Mayne as sole Commissioner until his death in 1868. The sentiments expressed in the 'Nine Principles' reflect those contained in the 'General Instructions', first published in 1829, which were issued to every member of the Metropolitan Police, especially the emphasis on prevention of crime as the most important duty of the police. Reith notes that Rowan and Mayne's conception of a police force was 'unique in history and throughout the world because it derived not from fear but almost exclusively from public co-operation with the police, induced by them designedly by behaviour which secures and maintains for them the approval, respect and affection of the public' (p. 140).

The Nine Principles of Policing

1. To prevent crime and disorder, as an alternative to their repression by military force and severity of legal punishment.

2. To recognise always that the power of the police to fulfil their functions and duties is dependent on public approval of their existence, actions and behaviour and on their ability to secure and maintain public respect.

3. To recognise always that to secure and maintain the respect and approval of the public means also the securing of the willing co-operation of the public in the task of securing observance of laws.

4. To recognise always that the extent to which the co-operation of the public can be secured diminishes proportionately the necessity of the use of physical force and compulsion for achieving police objectives.

5. To seek and preserve public favour, not by pandering to public opinion; but by constantly demonstrating absolutely impartial service to law, in complete independence of policy, and without regard to the justice or injustice of the substance of individual laws, by ready offering of individual service and friendship to all members of the public without regard to their wealth or social standing, by ready exercise of courtesy and friendly good humour; and by ready offering of individual sacrifice in protecting and preserving life.

6. To use physical force only when the exercise of persuasion, advice and warning is found to be insufficient to obtain public co-operation to an extent necessary to secure observance of law or to restore order, and to use only the minimum degree of physical force which is necessary on any particular occasion for achieving a police objective.

7. To maintain at all times a relationship with the public that gives reality to the historic tradition that the police are the public and that the public are the police, the

police being only members of the public who are paid to give full time attention to duties which are incumbent on every citizen in the interests of community welfare and existence.

8. To recognise always the need for strict adherence to police-executive functions, and to refrain from even seeming to usurp the powers of the judiciary of avenging individuals or the State, and of authoritatively judging guilt and punishing the guilty.

9. To recognise always that the test of police efficiency is the absence of crime and disorder, and not the visible evidence of police action in dealing with them.

Notes

Robert Skidelsky

1   Quoted in Macpherson, W., *The Stephen Lawrence Inquiry*, CM 4262-I, London: The Stationery Office, February 1999, p. 20. (Kent Report, para 14.28.)

2   Macpherson, *The Stephen Lawrence Inquiry*, CM 4262-I, p. 33.

3   Macpherson, *The Stephen Lawrence Inquiry*, CM 4262-I, p 16.

4   Macpherson, *The Stephen Lawrence Inquiry,* CM4262-I, para. 19.34, pp. 145-46.

5   Macpherson, *The Stephen Lawrence Inquiry,* CM4262-I, para. 19.37, p. 146.

6   Macpherson, *The Stephen Lawrence Inquiry,* CM4262-I, para. 19.38, p. 146.

John G.D. Grieve & Julie French

1   Where the personal pronouns 'I' and 'me' are used they refer to John Grieve.

2   Copyrighted material by Andrea Cork.

3   The Rt. Hon. The Lord Scarman, OBE, 'Report to the Rt. Hon. William Whitelaw CH, MC, MP, Secretary of State for the Home Department, on the Brixton Disorders of 10-12 April 1981', London: HMSO, November 1981, p. 65.

4   'The Brixton Disorders of 10-12 April 1981', 1981, p. 127.

5   Hoew, D., *From Bobby to Babylon: Blacks and the British Police*, London: Race Today Publications, 1988.

6   'The Brixton Disorders of 10-12 April 1981', 1981, p. 1.

7   Oakley, R., 'Institutional Racism and Police Service Delivery', quoted in Macpherson, W., *The Stephen Lawrence Inquiry*, London: The Stationery Office, February 1999, para. 6.31.

8   Oakley, 'Institutional Racism and Police Service Delivery', 1999, para. 6.32.

9 Neill, L.J., Industrial Cases Report, The Incorporated Council of Law Reporting for England and Wales, 1992, 516.

10 Industrial Cases Report, The Incorporated Council of Law Reporting for England and Wales, 1982, 132.

11 Industrial Relations Law Report, Industrial Relations Society, 1991, 264.

12 Macpherson, *The Stephen Lawrence Inquiry*, 1999, para. 6.34.

13 Macpherson, *The Stephen Lawrence Inquiry*, 1999, para. 6.39.

14 Burke, J.L., *Burning Angel*, London: Orion, 1995.

15 *The Guardian*, 14 October 1999.

16 Paul Barker, Senior Fellow of the Institute of Community Studies, *The Evening Standard*, 23 July 1999.

17 *The Sunday Telegraph*, 18 July 1999.

18 *The Guardian*, 22 March 1999.

19 Wilson, P., 'Institutional change', *Police Review*, 3 September 1999.

Michael Ignatieff

1 'Recommendations. Definition of racist incident 12', Macpherson, W., *The Stephen Lawrence Inquiry*, CM 4262-I, London: The Stationery Office, February 1999, p. 328.

David G. Green

1 Quoted in Kelling, G. and Coles, C., *Fixing Broken Windows*, New York: Free Press, 1996, p. 106. (The version of the principles quoted by Kelling refers to 'race and social standing', whereas the version in the Metropolitan Police archives says 'wealth and social standing'. The most salient social division in the 1820s was social class and the term 'race' was probably a later addition. Either way, the central concern is with equality before the law.)

2   *Race and the Courts: A Short Practical Guide for Judges*, Judicial Studies Board, 1999.

3   Sowell, T., *Preferential Policies*, New York: William Morrow, 1990, p. 14.

4   Sowell, *Preferential Policies*, p. 150.

5   Macpherson, W., *The Stephen Lawrence Inquiry*, CM 4262-I, London: The Stationery Office, February 1999, p. 51.

6   Sowell, *Preferential Policies*, p. 15.

7   *Daily Telegraph*, 13 June 2000.

Independence

The Institute for the Study of Civil Society is a registered educational charity (No. 1036909). The ISCS is financed from a variety of private sources to avoid over-reliance on any single or small group of donors.

All publications are independently refereed and referees' comments are passed on anonymously to authors. All the Institute's publications seek to further its objective of promoting the advancement of learning. The views expressed are those of the authors, not of the ISCS.